AF320554

COPING WITH CRISIS

Pull your company back from the brink

Written by Véronique Bronckart
Translated by Emma Hanna

COPING WITH CRISIS

- **Problem:** what material and human resources should you use in order to cope with a crisis and resolve it quickly?
- **Uses:** minimise the immediately harmful effects, stabilise the situation and take any necessary lessons on board in order to prevent subsequent crises.
- **Professional context:** crisis anticipation and management, conflict resolution, management, human resources.
- **FAQs:**
  - What constitutes a crisis situation?
  - Who is likely to have to face crisis situations?
  - Who should sound the alarm?
  - How can I resolve a crisis situation?
  - How should I communicate during a crisis?
  - Will I be able to deal with a crisis situation without having previously drawn up a crisis management plan?
  - What are the potential psychological consequences of mismanaging a crisis?
  - What mistakes should be avoided in order to

minimise the damage?

Any company, whether it is a multinational corporation or a local business and no matter what sector it is active in, can find itself with a crisis on its hands. Crisis situations, which can sometimes arise completely unexpectedly, damage the company's reputation and efficiency, and in a worst-case scenario they can even lead to bankruptcy. Knowing how to properly manage a crisis is therefore essential in order to restore an atmosphere that fosters trust and security for the company's employees, directors, suppliers and clients, and to get the business back on track.

Regardless of whether the crisis is financial, social or environmental in nature, and whether it has arisen due to internal or external factors, resolving it will require substantial management skills in order to manage the resulting stress, react quickly and intelligently, communicate properly, and eventually take the necessary lessons from the experience on board so that the crisis does not repeat itself. Crisis management has become a crucial strategic tool for businesses.

In this guide, you will discover the different

stages of an effective risk management process, as well as learning how to take advantage of these kinds of situations and how to identify risk factors more accurately. We will also analyse the importance of appropriate internal and external communication, press relations and the potential impact of social media. Protect your business from threats by mastering the art of crisis management!

HANDLING A CRISIS: THE BASICS

SPOTTING A CRISIS

What is a crisis situation?

A crisis situation can be defined as circumstances which threaten a company's goals or survival and which make snap decisions necessary. Whether or not a situation constitutes a crisis also depends on its seriousness and its impact on the company. As such, difficult circumstances which nevertheless do not have serious consequences for the company or for its associates would not be defined as a crisis. These situations can sometimes be predicted, but not always. After all, even though potential problems can sometimes be predicted by carrying out an internal analysis of the company which allows the various risk factors at hand to be identified, external risk factors are generally impossible to predict.

Crisis situations can arise from various interconnected sources, including economic, politi-cal, institutional, social, ethical, technical, legal and media-related fields. As such, they can be natural, technological, environmental or human in nature, and have incredibly disparate origins. As shown in the diagram below, these different factors are interrelated and both influence and are influenced by the company. As such, an event which affects one of these sectors can have direct repercussions for the company or for another factor which will then have an impact on another, and another, and so on, causing a domino effect.

Potential causes of a crisis

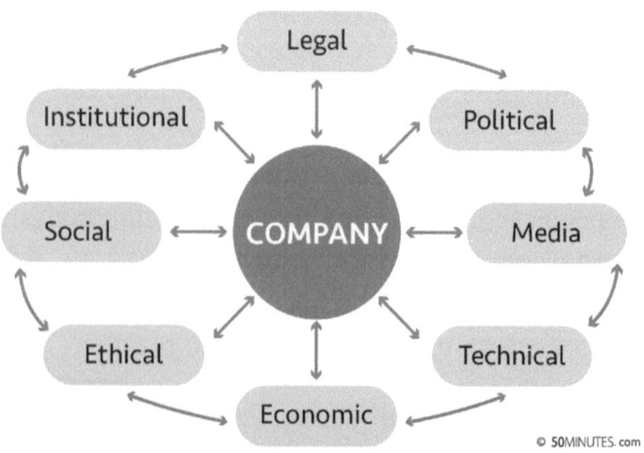

Companies face many problems on a daily basis. These problems can usually be resolved quickly, but sometimes the situation will continue to spiral out of control. Once the risk factors have been identified and a risk management policy has been put in place, it becomes a "potential crisis situation". If these factors are observed to be multiplying unchecked, then a "crisis situation" will be declared. This process generally comprises several stages, as outlined in the following diagram:

Crisis management process

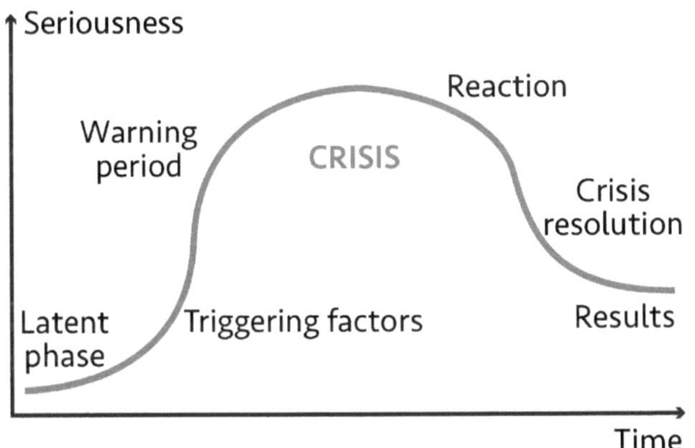

Risk factors

When multiple risk factors accumulate, this will result in a crisis situation. These risk factors may be internal or external in nature, and will each have an effect on the others. Learn how to identify them so that you can predict their consequences more accurately.

Risk factors

External factors	Internal factors
• Aggressive competition. • New legislation which makes internal restructuring necessary. • Relocation or location mergers. • Information which is harmful to the company's image (scandal, bad publicity). • Threats towards staff by a client or a supplier. • Multiple cancelled orders. • Closure of an important supplier (strike, bankruptcy).	• Irreversible decision-making errors. • Internal regulation which is too strict or imprecise. • Lack of communication, rumours. • Lack of foresight at the executive level. • Reshuffles or redistribution of the workload. • Services being phased out. • Technical faults or malfunctions. • Human error. • Understaffing, overwork. • Conflict.

What consequences will the company face?

Whether the crisis has arisen due to a poor decision, general unrest or an unforeseeable external event, it will always cause upheaval and instability. If the crisis is not controlled, it can have direct effects on the key players in the company. In fact, depending on how well-informed they are, these individuals may feel that their position is being threatened, create rumours or feel like they have been cut adrift, which will cause motivation to fall and will have a knock-on effect on the company's profitability and finances. As such, good communication with all employees is critical in these kinds of circumstances in order to reassure and support them and to get them involved in the resolution process. Depending on the type of crisis the company is facing, the repercussions may also affect the company's supplies or sites (and cause production to slow down or halt), harm the company's image or, in a worst-case scenario, lead to layoffs and bankruptcy.

PREVENTING A CRISIS

Preventing a crisis means being capable of responding and reacting to unforeseen circumstances and, in some cases, being able to abandon conventional beliefs and methods in order to adapt to the new situation. In order to maximise the effectiveness of your response, you will need a well-prepared crisis management process which aims to identify risk factors, for example through audits, and to take specific measures in order to minimise the potential repercussions for the company.

Identifying company goals and risks

The first essential step involves identifying the company's goals. Once they have been established, it then becomes possible to discern the factors which could hinder the pursuit of these goals and the factors which are not a threat. Preventative measures should only be applied to factors which pose a genuine risk.

In order to identify potential threats, you will need to analyse the company's vulnerabilities. Although you can establish a monitoring or crisis management committee to carry out this analysis, truly comprehensive results can only be obtained if the company undergoes an external audit, as this will provide a more global, objective overview of the situation. This study should cover all of the parameters related to the company's internal and external operations, evaluate its strengths and weaknesses and classify all possible risks according to their seriousness and their probability. This approach serves as an excellent guideline when planning preventative actions.

Mapping risk factors

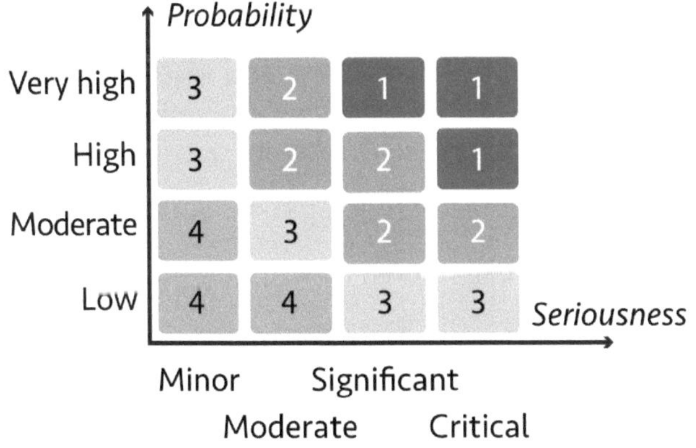

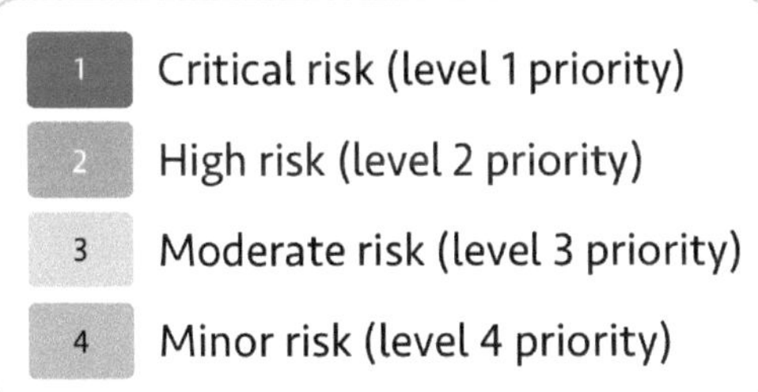

The crisis management plan

Once the risks have been identified, a crisis management plan which encompasses all of the strategies and resources which are appropriate for the seriousness of the situation at hand should be put in place. This will involve:

- setting up basic warning and victim management procedures (who activates them and how?);
- creating an effective, specific communication plan;
- creating a business continuity plan;
- identifying the members of the crisis management committee and their roles;
- training the company's spokesperson in media relations;
- preparing staff using simulation exercises.

This information can be recorded in a written document (the crisis management plan), which will only include the essential information in order to maximise its effectiveness. This plan should be updated regularly so that it can be used when it is needed, and should therefore address every variety of potential crisis (legal, financial, etc.). At this stage in the preventative process, you should also develop strategies to limit the impact of collateral damage in the event of a crisis. These strategies should cover the following factors:

- protecting the company's image by informing suppliers and clients about the company's values and the measures which have been adopted to ensure that they are respected;
- reducing the impact of the media on your staff by keeping them apprised of the situation in order to avoid misunderstandings;
- helping the families involved by providing them with psychological support.

The communication plan

Although it is only one part of your overall plan, it is essential to have a crisis communication plan (CCP), and this step should not be neglected. In order to create an effective plan, bear the following factors in mind:

- identify the various targets (media, general public, employees, authorities, clients);
- define the communication goals and appropriate resources for each target;
- specify what each measure involves (topics addressed, key messages, author, frequency, etc.);
- establish the methods which should be used to monitor the results of these actions.

The business continuity plan

The business continuity plan (BCP) encompasses all the procedures and operations which allow the company to continue operating during the crisis and therefore to guarantee a certain degree of financial security. It consists of two sections (depending on the company and the type of incident involved):

- an **IT continuity plan (ICP)**, which focuses on ensuring that the IT system remains operational;
- an **operational continuity plan (OCP)**, which focuses on operating procedures and professional demands (meaning the activity that gives the company value).

By ensuring that your clients continue to receive the services or deliveries they need, you will earn their trust and prove that you are reliable. Furthermore, seeing that the company is doing everything it can to remain operational will reassure employees and boost their motivation. The BCP should be adapted to respond to the situation at hand:

- for a crisis related to a shortage of supplies, the plan should include options such as the use of alternative raw materials or a new supplier so that production can continue;
- for an environmental crisis (flooding, fire, etc.), the plan should take the need for additional operational resources during the repairs process into account.

RPO AND RTO

The BCP should also include the recovery point objective (RPO) and recovery time objective (RTO). The former refers to the time frame between the incident and the last time the company's data was saved, and quantifies the maximum amount of data that can be deemed an acceptable loss. The latter refers to the length of time that the company is not operational, and quantifies the maximum acceptable downtime. These two parameters must be established to ensure that the BCP is effective.

Preparing these different plans will allow you to minimise the errors made when making decisions under pressure and to gain precious time when a crisis arises.

The crisis management committee

Crisis resolution is a process which is heavily influenced by the nature, cause and seriousness of the crisis in question. However, one element remains constant: the need to mobilise key players who can help to find solutions. This is the purpose of a crisis management committee, which should consist of:

- a crisis manager (who chairs the committee);
- a coordinator who acts as the liaison between the committee and the rest of the company;
- a head of communication;
- a psychologist (depending on the seriousness of the crisis);
- specialists who work in the relevant field (legal expert, environmental expert, scientist, IT security supervisor, etc.).

This team should be available at all times and able to mobilise quickly. As such, they should receive training in how to deal with a wide variety of situations.

RESOLVING THE CRISIS

Reaction time

When a crisis arises, it is imperative to react swiftly and to accurately assess the situation so that the seriousness of the crisis becomes immediately apparent. This will allow quick, judicious decisions to be made and prevent stress from setting in. The crisis management committee should be assembled as soon as possible and should ensure that any external agents (advisors, legal experts) are able to coordinate with staff in order to make a well-organised, concerted, coherent effort to deal with the crisis. Any action taken to tackle the crisis will only be effective if it is taken quickly. In fact, crisis management can best be described as a race against time. Depending on the seriousness of the crisis, the committee may also recommend that those who find the situation stressful, whether they are members of staff or committee members, should receive counselling in order to limit collateral damage.

The importance of communication

One of the most crucial aspects of good crisis management is communication. Clear internal communication is vital, as this will reduce reaction time and reassure employees. External communication via the media and social networks is also essential, as this will keep the public informed and help to protect the company's image.

- **Internal communication:** employees are often the first victims in any crisis situation. As such, transparency should be central to your internal communication strategy in order to avoid risks and to prevent employees from hearing the bad news on the television or on the grapevine. Giving them a clear understanding of the situation at the earliest possible opportunity will strengthen the sense of community within the company and preserve your employees' trust, which will prove vital at critical junctures. Internal communication also plays an important role in allowing the measures decided upon by the crisis management committee to be put into practice more quickly and easily. The committee should use reliable tools such as telephones (landlines or mobiles), emails, the crisis management plan and a full list of contact details for any individual affected by the crisis to communicate with the rest of the company. In some cases, committees create their own internal web platform, which is an area set aside for any communication within the group. It may also include visual elements (charts, graphs, tables) which allow users to monitor how the crisis is developing in real time, to view the decisions and actions which have been put in place and their rate of progress, and to see any warning signals that are set off when deadlines are not met. Employees should also be informed of any successful measures as soon as their effectiveness can be confirmed in order to restore their motivation and their belief in the company's potential.

- **External communication:** this is essential in order to keep the outside world (clients, suppliers, partners, the general public, associates, etc.) apprised of the situation within the company and to protect the company's image. This means that it is important to cultivate a good relationship with the media, as it is the media who will relay information to the public. As such, you should ensure that all the information you release is not only correct, but also casts the company in the best possible light, as it is essential to avoid tarnishing your company's reputation too much. Social networks give you the chance to relay the facts regularly and at a moment's notice, allowing you to forestall gossip and false information while reassuring the public and your clients. Using social media also allows you to keep an eye on the company's online reputation, which will allow you to keep up to date with any news about the company that is being circulated, and will give you a chance rectify the situation if necessary.

<u>**Case study: efficient crisis communication**</u>

In February 2013, the brand Findus realised that its beef lasagnes actually contained horsemeat following a series of quality checks. The company reacted immediately, using an effective crisis communication plan which was based on three key points:

- the brand made the scandal public knowledge and showed that it was taking the crisis and its clients' welfare seriously by recalling its products;
- it ensured that all of its communication was totally transparent and carried out DNA tests on all of its products that contained beef;
- it took the consumers' side, and positioned itself on the same level as them (as victims) by laying the blame on the suppliers.

Positive communication attitudes to adopt in crisis situations

Pitfalls to avoid	Positive attitudes
• Refusing to take responsibility and accusing others. • Playing all your cards at once. • Lying. • Keeping quiet, as this risks fuelling the media's imagination. • Contradicting yourself. • Waffling. • Releasing unconfirmed information.	• Acknowledging and accepting the crisis. • Showing empathy towards the victims. • Being transparent, within reason. • Talking about the future and the measures taken to resolve the crisis. • Keeping things in perspective and staying positive.

EMERGING FROM THE CRISIS

Never assume that your work is finished once the worst is over and the company has emerged from the crisis. This is a critical stage which will determine what comes next, as well as serving to rebuild the trust of your staff, clients, suppliers, the authorities and the media. It is also a time to take the lessons you have learned during the experience on board to prevent the same thing happening again in the future.

As with all events which affect the company, it is wise to draw up an overview by debriefing all those involved and identifying areas for improvement. It is a particularly good idea to carry out an audit after the crisis, using the initial audit as a base, defining the pre-existing risk factors which still apply and adapting the crisis management process in order to further reduce both the likelihood of a similar situation arising again in the future and the potential impact on the company. Based on this new audit, the crisis management committee will create a new crisis management process by adapting the planned preventative measures.

Finally, the company should use this experience to bounce back and revitalise itself, as learning from past mistakes will lead to growth and improvement. Try setting a new objective and drawing up a new action plan for achieving it in order to get your business back on track and motivate your employees.

The qualities of a good crisis manager

- Being optimistic – if the crisis is handled properly, the outcome may well be positive.
- Being aware of the situation and not burying your head in the sand, as this will not improve matters. Confront the problem head-on.
- Expecting the unexpected and chain reactions.
- Taking a step back and viewing things objectively.
- Demonstrating common sense and sound judgement.
- Acting calmly – if you start to panic, your employees will follow your example, so keep your cool.

TOP TIPS

- **Look for new suppliers.** Never rely on just one, as this will create significant risks for your company if that supplier has problems. Prepare a contingency plan by contacting two or three different suppliers. It is important to always keep an eye out for new partners who could turn out to be key allies at a critical juncture.
- **Make sure that your communication (internal and external) is transparent.** This will ensure that information does not get garbled. It is also essential that the crisis management committee approves all decisions before employees or the media are informed of them. Finally, it is important to formulate all communication clearly, so that the public and employees can understand everything (avoid jargon), but it should also be honest, empathetic and humble.
- **Cultivate your working relationships and public image.** The company's credibility and capacity to emerge from the crisis depend on it. Projecting the image of a strong, confident

brand during the conflict resolution phase will help you to hold on to the majority of your clients. Conversely, neglecting it will leave your company vulnerable to being abandoned by its clients, who will defect to one of your competitors.

- **Unite all of your staff through a crisis resolution project.** Troubled times, like prosperous times, are good opportunities to strengthen the bonds between those working for the company. Plus, encouraging employees to get involved and show their solidarity will increase your chances of turning the situation around.
- **Do not succumb to stress and panic.** You will not be able to tackle a crisis situation properly if you cannot manage your stress levels. Extreme stress can lead to panic, mistakes, and hasty, ill-advised decisions, which will hinder your attempts to resolve the situation and ultimately lead to failure. Being able to foresee the crisis will take a great weight off your shoulders at the first hurdle. To avoid giving in to stress, surround yourself with experts who are familiar with the situation. You should also keep things in perspective and take deep breaths when you feel anxious. It may also

be a good idea to take a stress management training course, consult a coach who can help you to prepare for these kinds of situations or practice relaxation techniques such as yoga or sophrology. The members of the crisis management committee should also mentally prepare themselves, as they will be on the front lines and will therefore be exposed to the highest levels of stress.

- **Ask yourself how the company could benefit from the experience.** The French economist Jean Monnet (1888-1979) once said: "People only accept change when they are faced with necessity, and only recognise necessity when a crisis is upon them." A crisis situation could be a chance to reorient the company and breathe new life into it.
- **Learn from your mistakes.** After the crisis has passed, take the time to draw up an overview and analyse the way it was handled. Evaluate the damage, identify the risk factors which are still in play and try to neutralise them. It is also highly advisable to use a different evaluation method from the previous time so that the preventative measures can be adapted and improved.

- **Always be prepared.** If you only remember one of these tips, make sure it is this one! Develop action strategies to tackle all of the potential risk factors. For example, one strategy that could be used to deal with human factors is to keep a list of the contact details of any people who have the same skills as your employees and who could replace them in case of absence. For technical risks, try to anticipate your team's potential training needs.

FAQS

WHAT CONSTITUTES A CRISIS SITUATION?

A crisis situation is triggered when an event threatens the company's goals, image, operations or survival. These periods cause great upheaval, which in turn generates confusion. Some examples of crisis situations include toxic leaks, raw materials becoming unavailable, strikes or the company's reputation being damaged by media criticism.

WHO IS LIKELY TO HAVE TO FACE CRISIS SITUATIONS?

Any company or business can find itself in a crisis situation. However, crises may not necessarily be economic or environmental in nature – they can be caused by a great variety of different internal and external factors. For example, a dissatisfied customer posting a scathing review online could trigger a crisis situation for a small local business.

WHO SHOULD SOUND THE ALARM?

Any employee who observes a potential problem which could cause a serious crisis should alert their manager. It will then be the manager's responsibility to sound the alarm. Depending on the crisis management committee's structure, the chairperson or the head of communication will send out a more widespread alert to the rest of the staff and to the media.

HOW CAN I RESOLVE A CRISIS SITUATION?

The best way to manage a crisis situation is to be prepared for it. This means that you will have to put a great deal of work in beforehand, particularly by carrying out an analysis of the company in order to identify internal and external risk factors, which will enable you to put preventative measures in place by creating a crisis management committee and drawing up various action plans. Be patient and do not panic; crises take time to resolve. Stay optimistic and do not give up, and you will soon see the light at the end of the tunnel.

HOW SHOULD I COMMUNICATE DURING A CRISIS?

Communication should be comprehensible to everyone and should generally avoid jargon that could cause confusion or misunderstandings. Announcements should be made as soon as possible after the crisis arises, and in the case of a potential crisis, it is highly advisable to warn staff in advance, before the crisis is officially declared, in order to forestall any rumours that might begin to spread and exacerbate the situation. Ideally, communication should be regular and should take the way events are unfolding into account. Announcements can be made via the media or social networks, or during meetings with staff or with representatives for the parties involved (consumers, locals, ecologists, etc.).

WILL I BE ABLE TO DEAL WITH A CRISIS SITUATION WITHOUT HAVING PREVIOUSLY DRAWN UP A CRISIS MANAGEMENT PLAN?

A crisis management plan is an incredibly useful tool and will contribute enormously to a successful outcome. If you have not drawn up a plan beforehand, you will need to possess the necessary skills to face emergencies head-on, have readily available lists of contacts, be able to bring together a group of experts on short notice and make swift, effective decisions. Crisis situations are usually unsettling and highly stressful, so it can be difficult to remain objective and manage the situation to the best of your ability. This is why having a crisis management plan is so highly recommended. However, if you have neglected to create one, it does not mean that your company is doomed from the outset, so long as it and its employees have the resources they need to bounce back.

WHAT ARE THE POTENTIAL PSYCHOLOGICAL CONSEQUENCES OF MISMANAGING A CRISIS?

Mismanaging a crisis can have noticeable psychological consequences on the members of the crisis management committee and on the company's staff. The seriousness of these consequences may range from lack of motivation, loss of concentration or irritability to depression or even burnout. As such, it is important to take these individuals seriously and to provide any specialised psychological support that they may need.

WHAT MISTAKES SHOULD BE AVOIDED IN ORDER TO MINIMISE THE DAMAGE?

In order to limit the potential damage, it is crucial that you do not attempt to hide the reality of the situation from the company's staff in order to prevent any rumours that could aggravate the situation from spreading; burying your head in the sand will not solve any problems. Furthermore, failure to take the repercussions for your employees' mental health and the company's finances into account could have serious consequences.

OVER TO YOU

CRISIS MANAGEMENT LOG

You can use this log as a guide for the various stages of the crisis.

Crisis management log

Audit/ Analysis	Who is carrying out the audit? What method are they using? What contextual factors (internal or external factors) have been taken into account? When should the analysis be carried out?
Internal risk factors (also applicable to external risk factors)	What kinds of factors have been identified (technical, human, other)? How serious/likely are they? How could they be dealt with? What actions and reactions relating specifically to each factor could be used in a crisis?
Creation of a crisis management committee	Who are the committee members? What are their roles? How does the committee work? What warning systems and crisis management procedures have been put in place? What means of communication does the committee use? Does the committee meet regularly or only during crises?

Creation of a crisis management plan	What is the communication plan? (What is each person's role? How do they carry it out?) Have the necessary contact lists been created? Has a business continuity plan been drawn up?
Preventative actions	What actions have been planned? What schedule should they follow? Have any training courses, psychological preparation or drills been planned?
Crisis management	Who triggers the alert? How much time can be set aside for reacting and making decisions? What schedule should the planned actions follow? What means of communication should be used? Is any external support (experts) included in the plan? What kind of support will be available for the people involved? What is the intended result?
Feedback	Were effective decisions made? What could be improved?

New audit	Once it has been completed, compare it to the previous audit.
New crisis prevention and management action plan	How does it differ from the previous plan? Is the company prepared for another crisis?

We want to hear from you!
Leave a comment on your online library
and share your favourite books on social media!

FURTHER READING

BIBLIOGRAPHY

* Gorius, A. (2013) Réussir sa com' de crise : 5 exemples à la loupe. *Journal du net*. [Online]. [Accessed 2 November 2017]. Available from: <http://www.journaldunet.com/management/direction-generale/communication-de-crise>

* Loury, C. (1999) *Management des situations de crise. De la stagnation à la croissance*. Paris: FMK Consulting.

* Maisonneuve, D., Saouter, C. and Char, A. (2001) *Communication en temps de crise*. Québec: Presses de l'Université du Québec.

* Pardini, G. (2010) *La gestion de crise*. Paris: INHESJ.

* Gestion de crise. (No date) *Réagir à la crise : les principes-clés*. [Online]. [Accessed 2 November 2017]. Available from: <http://www.gestionde-crise.com/reagir-a-la-crise-les-principes-cles>

ADDITIONAL SOURCES

* Crandall, W., Parnell, J. and Spillan, J. (2013) *Crisis Management: Leading in the New Strategy Landscape*. 2nd edition. Thousand Oaks: Sage Inc.

- Fink, S. (2002) *Crisis Management: Planning for the Inevitable*. Revised edition. Lincoln: iUniverse.